COUPLES WHO ARGUE

Allen Ross

Illustrations by Greg Knepp.
Front cover by Emily Fotis.
Layout and back cover by Charlie Einhorn.

Published by Allen Ross Publications.

ISBN 978-057-808-4923

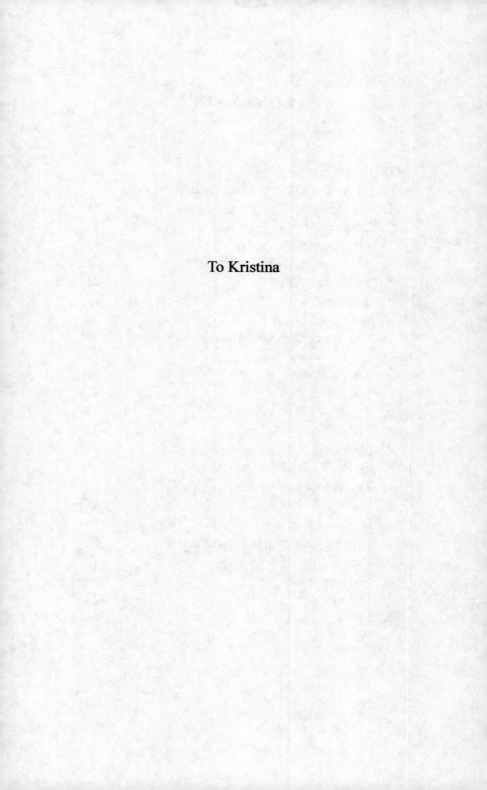

To Kristina

CONTENTS

Author's Overview

Arguing is pointless. You are verbally abusing each other and the very process of arguing prevents you from resolving the disagreement. Arguing can wear you down and gradually erode the intimate connection that is the core of your relationship. In my own counseling practice, I have found it to be the primary problem for many couples – not *what* you are arguing about, but the process of arguing *itself.*

There are several meanings for the word "argument". What I am addressing is a disagreement that has become nasty. I will get more specific as the topic unfolds.

To understand the dynamics of an argument, it will first be necessary to understand the nature of criticism.

People often have negative thought below the surface of the mind. It is name-calling. It can be directed inward against yourself or outward against others. It is this name-calling that I will be referring to as "criticism".

Whether the criticism is directed at yourself or your partner, it is *deceptive*. Since it operates secretly below the surface, you are usually not aware of it. But from there it can cause you to be hard to please, judgmental, impatient, defensive, angry, sarcastic, intolerant, depressed…the list goes on and on.

Parts I and II of this book give a clear understanding of how criticism operates. Part III helps you to recognize it in the moment, and Part IV gives you the strategy to reduce and eventually stop it. Once you understand criticism, it will be easy to follow Part V which lays out the basics of anger. You are then ready for Part VI, which explains the dynamics of an argument, how it starts, how it escalates, and how to avoid it in the first place.

Reducing your inner criticism is a gradual process. By contrast, preventing arguments is quick, immediate work. So, while an understanding of criticism is an essential prerequisite, your actual work to prevent arguments begins in Parts V and VI. However, the book progresses through a sequence of key concepts, making it necessary to read from beginning to end without jumping ahead.

On a more personal note, teaching couples how to prevent arguments combines everything I have been learning, developing and teaching for the past 34 years. I find the work very gratifying. If you both *want* to stop arguing, then you will find that the simple tools presented in these pages will help you to do just that… quickly. After just a few sessions, couples will typically return to my office pleasantly surprised. May you also experience that same pleasant surprise.

Allen Ross
September, 2012

PART I

THE ORIGINS
OF CRITICISM

one

THE PERILS OF CHILDHOOD

Childhood is an impressionable time. At birth you begin to receive a steady flow of messages about who you are in this new world. You tend to absorb these messages indiscriminately in the early years of your development.

These messages can be communicated verbally or non-verbally. Young children are very receptive to tone of voice, quality of touch, facial expression and gestures. A child can sense the parent's tenseness, tenderness, irritation, fear, warmth, emotional closeness and emotional distance. As time goes on, the child also becomes aware of the parent's expectations and disapproval.

Criticism against yourself originates during childhood in response to negative messages from one or both parents (or other significant adults). The following list gives some examples of the more overt behavior patterns that can communicate these messages to children.

not enough warmth
emotional distance
not enough full attention
not enough love
not enough encouragement
few compliments
conditional love
criticism
sharp tone of voice
anger
intimidation
being hard to please
being over-restrictive
having high expectations
favoritism
abuse

These behavior patterns in parents are usually brought on by their own inner criticism. Children, in a manner of speaking, inherit the process of criticism from their parents. But there is no blame implied. Generation after generation, we are all victims of this unfortunate legacy.

two

INTROJECTION

Adults generally question new information. They "chew it up" before swallowing it. What they do eventually swallow will be digested and assimilated. It becomes their own. Children, on the other hand, don't typically question new information, they swallow it whole. As a result, it remains inside of them undigested. It is foreign.

To swallow information whole is called introjection. It's how children learn. They tend to introject their parent's values, beliefs, opinions and traits. Back in elementary school during the Eisenhower-Stevenson presidential race, I can remember some rather loud (and occasionally physical) political debates out on the playground. No doubt, we were all expressing the opinions we had introjected from our parents.

Martha is 32 years old. When she questions her busy doctor about the medication he has prescribed, she is chewing the information before swallowing. It takes a certain amount of aggressiveness to chew, to question information we are fed. Young children don't really have the "teeth" for it. (I borrow the analogy of eating from the work of Fritz Perls.)

Johnny is only five. He has just drawn a picture and wants his Dad to appreciate it. But Dad is watching TV and when Johnny takes the picture to him, Dad hardly notices, says "uh huh" and continues to watch his program. Johnny won't think about this and try to determine if it's Dad's problem or his own. Johnny just automatically (and unknowingly) absorbs that it is his own shortcoming. As he continues to introject such "information" about himself, he begins to feel not good enough. He begins to experience self-criticism.

As a child grows toward adolescence, he or she gradually develops the capacity to chew information before swallowing, and the process of introjection declines. The budding adolescent then begins to purge what has already been introjected and struggles for his or her *own* opinions, values and rules of behavior. This "adolescent rebellion" is a natural stage of development.

Still, we can only purge what we identify as foreign. Unfortunately, the negative messages about our self-worth settle *below* the surface so we don't notice them. As a result, we don't purge them. Once inside, they can remain with us for life, and form the basis for self-criticism.

three

THE "DEMON" METAPHOR

Throughout the rest of the book, I will be using the metaphor of a "demon" to characterize inner criticism. I chose this image because it accurately captures several key aspects of criticism in a single "picture". If you find this image difficult to use because it is too negative, then you might substitute another name such as enemy, inner critic or inner judge. Still, I chose this metaphor because I believe it is a fitting portrayal of a thought process that creates much harm.

For teaching purposes, I will initially be discussing criticism of your self, and later branch out to criticism of others. What follows are the three key aspects of the criticism process (the "demon").

AUTONOMOUS: The "demon" operates independently below the surface without your knowledge or consent. You don't choose to be attacked and generally do not even know that it is happening.

EXTERNAL: The "demon" is introjected, created from negative messages you swallowed as a child. As such, it is not a part of you but an invader from the outside. Emphasis on the introjected nature of criticism is the cornerstone of this metaphor. Even though the criticism comes from within, it is foreign in nature. You are, in a manner of speaking, being criticized by an external enemy.

NEGATIVE: The "demon" is completely malicious, being composed only of negative messages. It has no redeeming features whatsoever. The next section will further elaborate this aspect of criticism.

Using this metaphor will make it easier to step back and observe the criticism process within you.

At this point in the discussion, the term "self-criticism" is misleading because it implies that you criticize yourself. I will therefore switch to the more accurate term, "inner criticism". I will also be using the words "criticism" and "attack" interchangeably. Criticism, as I use the word, is simply name-calling.

And name-calling is a verbal attack. So, below the surface, the "demon"* is attacking you.

---

* The word "demon" will remain in quotes throughout the book to emphasize that it is only a metaphor. The quotes also serve as containment in deference to those who believe that the name carries the form.

four

THE "DEMON" IS ENTIRELY NEGATIVE

Childhood is a mixture of positive and negative experiences. Mary, age 4, is tired and has been in the supermarket with mom for ten minutes now, so she starts to whimper and fuss. Mom, not having a great day herself, finally gets irritated and threatens, "If you don't behave, I'm going to smack you." Mary's response might be to introject the message "I don't matter" even though at other times she receives clear messages that she does matter. The strength of Mary's "demon" will depend more on *patterns* of negative input than on isolated incidents.

Parents can love their children very much and still give negative messages. One of my clients related that she felt well loved as a child but still grew up with strong inner attack. Her parents had strict rules about what was "proper" and she vividly remembers how her mother's disapproval, communicated by a certain look, made her feel very guilty. So the "demon" forms in a mixed atmosphere, not a completely negative one. Yet it still turns out 100% malicious. The negative messages merge together, polarizing away from all that is positive in us. Made up only of these messages, the "demon" is pure, distilled malice.

Remember that the "demon" is foreign, it is not a *part* of you. It is not an aspect of your personality, or your "dark side", or your "critical parent", or a sub-personality. When a blight moves into a forest, it is not a characteristic of the trees, but an affliction. Likewise, inner attack is a blight on the human race, not a human characteristic. The "demon" is simply a disorder.

The "demon's" attack is a deep one. It is against your core self. To better understand the nature of this attack, we must consider the nature of the self. Ralph Waldo Emerson referred to a person's deepest nature as the "soul".

> "The soul in man... is not a faculty but a light... when it breathes through his will, it is virtue; when it flows through his affection, it is love."

This deepest nature I simply call your "self". Others refer to it as your "true self" or "inner self" or "higher self". But whatever the name, this is *who* you are. You are not your body, personality, thoughts or feelings. You *have* all of these. The you that has them is your self.

Your self is a source of goodness, love and joy. You are not born neutral, to be *made* good or bad by the whim of life's circumstances or the merit of your choices. You have no choice. At your core you are innately, irrevocably, completely good.

The more your self shines through, the more accurately your personality reflects *who* you truly are. The "demon's" attack darkens your mind and obstructs the light of your self. Your personality then reflects who you are less accurately.

Your self is always trying to emerge and shine more brightly in you. This emerging is called personal growth. The familiar comment, "I feel more myself today" is literally true. When you are more your self, you are happier, less inhibited, less judging and more loving.

six

SUMMARY

In Part I we introduced the concept of the "demon" as a metaphor for characterizing the process of criticism. We also discussed how the "demon" forms. We then went on to discuss the nature of the "demon" and the nature of the self.

PART II

THE ATTACK PROCESS

one

THE ATTACK OPERATES
IN THE SUBCONSCIOUS

Since inner criticism occurs in the subconscious, you are generally not aware of it. But you *feel* it. If you were being called a failure from below the surface, you probably would not notice it. You would simply *feel* like a failure.

The criticism operates secretly, in the dark, because it must. If you were to become aware of it, to shine the light on it, it would shrivel. The reason for this will become clear as our discussion continues.

two

THE HIT-WORD

The "demon's" attack is simply name-calling. The name it calls you is what I label a "hit-word". On the next page is a list of some of the more common hit-words. Scan the list. The words that "light up" are probably the ones your "demon" uses to attack you.

You introject the hit-word in childhood. At first it is just a generic feeling that something is wrong with you. As you get older and your vocabulary expands, you are able to name the feeling more accurately. If you were to enter adulthood with an introjected hit-word such as "inadequate", the *feeling* that you are inadequate could then affect you in a variety of situations for the rest of your life. And since the hit-word operates below the surface, you might never even know that it exists.

The most crucial feature of the hit-word is that it only attacks *who* you are. It is *you* that is inadequate, not something *about* you. It plays off of your shortcomings, mistakes and failures in order to strike at your core.

For example, the "demon" may use your performance at work as an excuse to call you a failure. But (and here is the deception) it does not mean that you are a failure professionally, it actually means that you are a failure *as a person.* This discussion continues in the next section.

SAMPLE HIT-WORDS

inferior	unlovable
inadequate	bad person
failure	don't deserve love
loser	unwholesome
worthless	toxic
not good enough	don't deserve happiness
don't measure up	low-life
not worth loving	degenerate
a nobody	undesirable
second rate	ominous
not worth much	scum
unacceptable	phony
pathetic	disgusting
defective	ass-hole (and other profanity)
something's wrong with me	harmful

three

THE EXCUSE

The "demon" is always looking for some excuse to attack you with a hit-word. Any excuse will do: your skinny legs, your lousy tennis serve, your low productivity, your lack of friends, that pimple on your nose, the remark you made, the test you failed, the money you lost, the water you spilled, and so on.

No matter what the excuse is *about*, the attack is always against *who* you are. So the "demon" will use the fact that Mark does not like you as an *excuse* to tell you that you are not worth liking. You, at your core, are not worth liking. That's the message. If not Mark, then the "demon" will find some other excuse for that message.

When you are down on yourself for causing your team to lose the big game, you are not simply feeling bad about how you played. That would only be regret. No, you are down on your *self*. The attack is not that you are worthless as a basketball player, it's that you are worthless as a *person*. The lousy game you played is just an excuse to deliver that message.

The "demon" simply waits for an opportunity. If you don't get called back for a second interview, it may call you a failure. If your deodorant fails, it may tell you that you are disgusting. Again, these hit-words usually do not become conscious thoughts. They operate below the surface so that you don't quite recognize the *thought* that you are disgusting, but simply *feel* that way.

In all cases, the target of an attack is your self.

four

SAMPLE ATTACKS

This section contains examples of hypothetical excuse/hit-word combinations. Usually you will be aware of the excuse but not the hit-word. The form is: Excuse *(hit-word)*.

I yelled at my son *(therefore I'm a bad person)*.
I'm fat *(therefore I'm not worth loving)*.
I don't have good clothes *(therefore I'm pathetic)*.
I'm not popular *(therefore I'm a nobody)*.
I don't make much money *(therefore I'm a loser)*.
She doesn't care about me *(therefore I'm not good enough)*.
I mess everything up *(therefore I'm worthless)*.
I masturbate *(therefore I'm disgusting)*.
I made the baby cry *(therefore I'm toxic)*.
I didn't get the job *(therefore I'm a failure)*.
I have thoughts of hurting people *(therefore I'm evil)*.

I'm unmarried *(therefore I'm inferior)*.
I'm not productive *(therefore I have no value)*.
I'm taking too long to learn this *(therefore I'm incompetent)*.

five

THE ATTACK IS ALWAYS A LIE

Since the target is always your self, the attack is saying that *who* you are is defective (or plug in any hit-word). But *who* you are cannot be defective. Any *aspect* of you can be defective (personality, behavior, skill level, body). But there can be no fact about you capable of making the core of your being defective. No one on the planet can be defective, or a loser, or worthless… as a person.

So the attack is always a lie.

six

THREE TYPES OF ATTACK

The "demon" can attack you in three different ways.

TYPE #1 ATTACK

This attack is aimed directly at you from the inside. Sarita is 47, has never been married and is not in a relationship. Her "demon" uses this as an excuse to tell her that she is not worth loving. Our discussion thus far has been about this form of the attack. It is the primary form. The next two types are projections of this first one.

TYPE #2 ATTACK

In addition to the attack being against your self, it can also turn against someone else. You criticize the other person. This is the type #2 attack. When your alcoholic brother-in-law gets his third DUI, you think that he is a real loser. The excuse is his third DUI, and the hit-word is "loser".

The type #2 attack is projection. Projection is attributing something about yourself to someone else. Suppose that you are angry inside and don't realize it. When your son storms into the house, you might think he is angry but he's actually just in a hurry. Your own unrecognized anger makes it easier to think your son is angry. That's projection.

Likewise, if the "demon" is calling you "worthless" below the surface and you don't realize it, you might, in turn, think that Tamara is worthless when she cancels plans with you at the last minute. That's the type #2 attack. As the attack projects outward, the hit-word might change to meet the circumstances. For instance, instead of worthless, you might think Tamara is an inconsiderate bitch.

Knowing that the type #2 attack is projection is simply for intellectual clarity. It has little to do with the actual strategy for stopping the attack.

The type #2 attack is usually conveyed indirectly, not as verbal name-calling. The following are a few examples.

1) <u>Tone</u> of <u>voice:</u> Most attacks are conveyed simply by tone of voice. When Maurice tells his son to clean up his room, and uses a certain tone of voice, there is an attack being delivered below the surface. Maurice is not aware of it, and does not intend it. If he were to pay attention to his tone of voice, he would be able to recognize the derogatory edge. If he were then to bring the language of the attack (the hit word) up to the surface, he might be horrified for expressing that to his son. His son is not consciously aware of the attack either, but only knows he dislikes how his father talks to him. There are many other nonverbal forms of the attack: voice inflection, a big sigh, rolling the eyes, a gesture, a cough, a certain look, raised eyebrows, a laugh, standing in someone's way, not holding the door – it all depends on the specific context. In these cases, the attack is implied, not spoken.

2) <u>Sarcasm:</u> This can be in fun with no malicious intent. More often, however, there is a nasty edge that signals the presence of a genuine attack.

3) "<u>Should</u>": This can be type #1 ("I should...") or type #2 ("You should..."). For every *should* there is an *or else*. If the *or else* is a hit-word, then the statement is an attack. For instance, if you say to Andre, "You should be more careful," that is an

attack if the invisible second half is "or else you are an ass." But if the second half is "or else you might hurt yourself," then it is merely a suggestion. "Must" functions similarly. Here are examples of type #1 attacks that can affect your entire life:

> I must be morally pure *(or else I'm depraved)*
> I must be attractive *(or else I'm not worth loving)*
> I must be special *(or else I'm insignificant)*

4) <u>The question</u>: In the right context, a question can be a disguised attack. "Why would you say that?" could mean "Anyone who would say that is a fool." "Where are you going?" could translate into "Only an inconsiderate prick would leave at a time like this." To expose the attack embedded in a question, turn it into a statement.

5) "<u>That</u>": If Tyler says "That's a stupid thing to say," he probably means that *you* are stupid for saying it.

6) "<u>Whatever</u>": Dad: "No, you are not leaving the house tonight." Chad: "Whatever!" (Translation: "Go to hell you evil destroyer of my happiness!") "Whatever" is not always an attack. It depends on what the person means by it.

7) <u>Insinuating</u>: Some verbal expressions are likely spots for attacks. Watch for sentences that begin with:

You always…
You never…
If you really…
Why don't you ever…
Even you…
Obviously…

There are many such expressions. In general, if you feel uncomfortable, you might be on the receiving end of an attack.

8) <u>Anger</u>: Anger at another person has a type #2 attack at its core. It is usually hidden below the surface unless there is verbal name-calling. More about this in Part V.

9) <u>Holding a grudge</u>: This is an ongoing resentment (type #2 attack) that runs in the background continuously. You won't notice it unless something brings to mind the person you resent.

10) <u>Disliking a person</u>: You can dislike a person without an attack, but it's a very common place for one. The attack toward that person lives inside of you, poisoning your mind.

11) <u>Having an attitude</u>: There are many ways to have an attitude. What you generally have is a type #2 attack. From below the surface, the attack creates that edge.

12) <u>Disappointment</u>: "I am disappointed in you" generally includes a hidden attack. Many parents unknowingly inflict this attack upon their kids.

13) <u>Prejudice</u>: This is a type #2 attack against an entire category of people, simply because they belong to that category. The hit-word is often a racial or ethnic slur.

14) <u>Hypothetical attack</u>: This is an imaginary attack. For instance, you imagine that Randy, who is house sitting for you, has forgotten to water your plants and you get mad at him for it. But you don't actually know that he has forgotten, and you are not actually mad at him. It's all fantasy, your mind is just wandering. Yet the attack within you is real and it affects your mood.

15) <u>Blaming inanimate objects</u>: When the door sticks and won't open and you growl and kick it, you are probably angry at the unfortunate door. It is somehow the door's fault. I read an article about a social worker who lost her license because she brought a gun to work and shot her computer. One

of my clients had manual dexterity problems and was at war with the physical world. Every time he fumbled with something he would get irritated at the object – the keys he dropped, the vitamins he spilled, the button that would not go into the buttonhole. The point here is that the type #2 attack can be directed at just about anything.

16) Imitating: For those of you who mimic others, if you do it in a derogatory manner, there is probably a hit-word below the surface.

17) Mental criticism: This is the most common form of the type #2 attack. You simply have a critical thought about someone without expressing it. For example, Monica walks into the room and you mentally criticize her for how she is dressed. Or you could be mentally attacking George all day for something he said to you that morning. In this case, the critical edge will not be in the tone of your voice but in the tone of your thoughts.

The type #2 attack has its own unique brand of deception. Even though it is directed at another, it is actually against you. The "demon" is *your* enemy, not the enemy of the other person. As such, its sole job is to make *you* feel worse. The attack magnifies your reaction to what you don't like, causing you to not like it even more. This puts you in a worse mood. Let me repeat that: when you criticize someone else, you put yourself in a worse mood. Notice this. Learn from it.

One of my clients used to get triggered 10-20 times a day. Every time he reacted, his mood would go down a notch. He would go from reaction to reaction, and without realizing it, his mood would usually be affected the whole day. Yet his reactions felt justified. He said he felt like he had the *right* to react. It took some work before he could recognize that, while his attacks were directed at other people (or things), his "demon" was actually causing *him* to suffer. As he got better at catching the attack before it could develop, his mood throughout the day steadily improved.

One final point: when you eliminate the type #2 attack, you don't become passive. You can still discipline your kids, strongly disagree with someone, dislike how a person acts, confront that person, and perhaps choose to give that person consequences. All of this can be done with no trace of an attack.

TYPE #3 ATTACK

When you are under a type #3 attack, you feel criticized by the other person. Instead of attacking you directly, the "demon" projects the attack out and it *seems* to come from the other person.

Jerry felt that Priscilla handed him the car keys too abruptly and so assumed she was upset with him for asking to borrow her car. When Alisha said it was late, and wanted to call it an evening, Ronald interpreted this to mean that she did not want to see him again. It sounded to Trent like Michael was just being polite when he laughed at his joke. When Julia told her mother that she quit her job, she thought her mother's look was disapproving. And so on – the possibilities are endless.

The language of the attack is usually below the surface. In the above paragraph, the hit-words might be:
1. Jerry felt that Priscilla thought he was a *user*,
2. Ronald didn't think Alisha considered him to be *good enough* for her,
3. Trent thought Michael saw him as *inferior*,
4. Julia believed that her mother thought she was *flaky*.

The type #3 attack can cause you to feel shy, self-conscious, inhibited, extra-sensitive, embarrassed, flustered, offended or hurt. It can lead you to misinterpret or misunderstand what someone has said. It could predispose you to feeling disliked, unwanted, unaccepted, ignored, discounted, unsupported, slighted, excluded, picked on or disrespected.

An interesting aspect of this attack is that it operates even when you actually *are* being criticized. If your "demon" were not activated, you would not take the attack personally. If Jenny were being blatantly nasty, you would simply think, "What's up with her?" You would not get defensive. It would seem like her problem, not yours. It might still be unpleasant, but *externally*, not *internally*. It would be like bad weather. You may not like it, but you don't take it personally.

The type #3 attack is what you assume others are thinking. It can be mild or strong, occasional or pervasive.

THREE TYPES OF ATTACK

seven

SUMMARY

In Part II we discussed how the attack operates. We described the hit-word, the excuse and the three types of attack. Part III is less systematic: it's a diverse collection of topics all related to helping you recognize attacks.

PART III

RECOGNIZING ATTACKS

one

TWO SOURCES OF DISTRESS

There are two primary sources of distress: the real world and the "demon". The real world is factual, so you must somehow deal with it. The "demon's" attack, on the other hand, is simply a lie. In that sense, I don't consider it part of the real world. And yet, the "demon" might actually cause as much distress as the real world (see page 80).

Throughout the day, the "demon" is constantly looking for some excuse to attack you. If you have car trouble, that's the real world and you won't feel great about it. The attack, that you are a "loser" for not having a better car in the first place, might then come in and make you feel even worse. That's the "demon's" job, to chime in and create additional distress. It's good at what it does.

A participant in one of my classes said that he had been stewing for several days over the poor job performance of an employee he supervises, mainly because the employee is a personal friend. It came out that he feels the person does not respect him (type #3) and is just using him (type #2). The real-world component of this is that he has a difficult situation to manage. The attacks do nothing but increase his distress.

When something real causes a problem, assume that the "demon" will try to make it worse. Your work is to sort it out, to recognize what part is real and what part is the attack.

Your goal is to react only to the real world.

two

KNOW YOUR PROFILE

How the "demon" operates in you can be very different from how it operates in someone else. Everyone has a unique profile.

Your "demon", in general, can range from mild to strong, and even this can vary from day to day, depending on other factors such as fatigue, stress and discomfort. What triggers you may not trigger the next person. The "demon" will use your own individual dislikes to trigger attacks against others, and your personal sensitivities to trigger attacks against yourself. And the strength of each attack will vary depending on the strength of the particular dislike or sensitivity.

The more familiar you are with your profile, the easier it will be to recognize attacks.

three

DISTRESS PATTERNS

Distress patterns are part of your profile. A distress pattern is an aspect of your personality created by the attack. The following are some examples of common distress patterns. I will generally give a strong version of the pattern, while your own version may be milder. Any hit-word I use to illustrate a pattern is just an example and not necessarily the one specific to you.

1) Self-conscious: You assume that someone is closely observing you and evaluating you negatively (type #3 attack). The result is that you are very aware of yourself, feeling awkward, inhibited and nervous.

2) Easily embarrassed: When you do or say something that you think might be construed by others as inappropriate, awkward or clumsy, you become

embarrassed. Your assumption is that they are reacting critically (type #3). If there were no attacks, embarrassment would not exist.

3) <u>Oversensitive</u>: You are prone to interpreting what others say or do as critical (type #3). This leads to exaggerating, misinterpreting and misunderstanding others. Your feelings are easily hurt. Others feel that they must be careful around you.

4) <u>Lacking</u> <u>trust</u>: You don't think people care enough about you (type #3) and will therefore hurt or betray you. As a result, you are suspicious of their motives or actions (type #2) and cautious in your dealings with them. In a love relationship, you hold back, fearing that you are not good enough (type #1) and that the other person will eventually want someone else or simply want to leave (type #3).

5) <u>Lacking</u> <u>confidence</u>: You feel that you do not measure up (type #1) and that others recognize it (type #3). So you assume you will not be chosen, hired or promoted. And if you were, you doubt that you would do a good enough job. In dating, you don't think the other person would want to go out with you (type #3). You tend to avoid taking chances, your motto being: "If I don't try, I won't fail." If you were to fail at something, the ensuing attack would cut you to shreds (type #1 or #3).

6) Passive: You lack confidence (see above) and so you let others make decisions for you. You also feel that if you asserted yourself, others would react negatively (type #3). You are an easy person to dominate.

7) The victim: You feel that the other person has low regard for you (type #3) and therefore mistreats you. As a result, you might feel anxious (type #3), helpless (type #1) or angry (type #2). If you were being mistreated and there were no attack operating, you would simply drop back, wonder what's up with the other person, and try to decide what to do about it. As an adult, you are only the emotional victim of your "demon", not the other person. There might still be some real-world distress, but it would be milder and caused by the actual situation, not an attack.

8) The martyr: You give to others but deny yourself. You deny yourself to highlight your giving, but also because you don't feel you deserve much (type #1). You give because you care, but feel unappreciated (type #3) and resent it (type #2).

9) Uncomfortable with compliments: Even though someone gives you a compliment, you fear that if you were to accept it, the person would think you are conceited (type #3). And you often feel that you

really don't deserve the compliment anyway (type #1). So you deflect it.

10) Impatient: Impatience is about not wanting anything to slow you down. When someone gets in your way, the type #2 attack will instantly fire. If the checkout clerk is making polite small talk with the customer ahead of you, the attack will create agitation. It is a habit that feeds on itself. The attacks make you more impatient. You will rush to get somewhere even though you are early. Another form of impatience is to be at odds with the physical world: the cellophane wrapper you can't remove from your new CD, the can opener that breaks, the traffic light that turns red just as you get to it, the computer that takes too long to do a simple task. There is an endless variety of ways the physical world can be uncooperative. Low-level attacks against inanimate objects can be ongoing, barely noticeable, and affect your mood the whole day (every day).

11) Jealous: You become suspicious very easily and accuse your partner of showing romantic interest in someone else (type #2). Your insecurity comes from feeling that you are not good enough for your partner (type #1) and assuming that he or she is looking for someone "better" (type #3). Being suspicious can, in some cases, be reasonable and need not entail jealousy.

12) <u>Guilty</u>: You feel that because of something you said, did or did not do, that you are a bad person (type #1). The "demon" takes your natural reaction of regret or remorse and twists it into guilt.

13) <u>Angry</u>: The type #2 attack is the core of anger against others. It's as if the attack itself burst into flame. The hit-word is usually hidden (which is typical for the type #2 attack) unless the conflict degenerates into name-calling. The type #1 attack is the core of anger against yourself. More on this in Part V.

14) <u>Critical</u>: You can readily pick out the faults, mistakes and weaknesses in others. Whether you mention it, harbor it inside, or tell another, the derogatory edge you feel identifies this as the type #2 attack.

15) <u>Resentful</u>: You dwell on what others have said or done to you, resenting them (type #2) and often imagining the retort you wish you had made (type #2). You are adept at holding a grudge (long-term resentment).

16) <u>Pessimistic</u>: You anticipate the worst because of your own inadequacy (type #1), the incompetence of others (type #2), others being against you (type #3) or bad luck (type #1).

17) <u>Depressed</u>: The real world can make you miserable. The "demon" will then play off of that misery and call you hopeless, worthless and useless (type #1). That turns you down into depression. Attack is the mainspring of depression. The tears that can accompany depression are often caused by the attack rather than real-world unhappiness.

18) <u>Defensive</u>: You feel criticized (type #3) and fire back indignantly (type #2).

19) <u>Argumentative</u>: You are quick to disagree. It's your tone of voice (type #2) that distinguishes you from someone who simply likes to debate. This pattern may include other patterns (e.g. critical, competitive, always right).

four

DISTRESS PATTERNS II:
COMPENSATIONS

Since the attack creates discomfort, you instinctively attempt to avoid it or compensate for it in various ways. Some of these compensations have become long-term patterns within your personality. The following are some typical patterns.

1) <u>Shy</u>: You fear that others will be critical of what you say or do (type #3) so you try to avoid being noticed.

2) <u>Entertaining</u>: You are at your best when you are the life of the party. But it tends to be your only speed. Below the surface, the attack tells you that you are of little consequence (type #1) and that others don't care very much (type #3). So you entertain because the positive attention momentarily dispels both attacks.

3) <u>Proud</u>: "I don't have to take this, it's beneath me."
Pride, in this sense, is the opposite of humility. It
is the attempt to build yourself up to neutralize the
attack that tears you down (type #1). There is also
the sort of pride that does not involve an attack, but
is simply feeling good about some accomplishment
or aspect of yourself.

4) <u>Hungry</u> <u>for</u> <u>attention</u>: You like to speak up in
groups and will tend to monopolize the discussion.
You have many ways of drawing attention to yourself
and will do extra work to gain recognition. Behind
this pattern you feel that others do not care about you
(type #3). You hunger for their attention because it
gives you the momentary feeling that they do care.

5) <u>Apologetic</u>: You try hard to not offend, or be
inappropriate, or be in the way, or be too loud, or be
too soft, or be too late, or be too early. You are quick
to apologize for the slightest infraction. You walk a
very thin line to avoid disapproval (type #3).

6) <u>Behind</u> <u>a</u> <u>wall</u>: Below the surface the attack says
that you are not worth loving (type #1). You believe
that if anyone really got to know you, they would
discover this (type #3). So you live behind a wall of
protection that prevents anyone from getting close
enough to hurt you.

7) <u>Always</u> <u>busy</u>: You rely on staying externally occupied. From work to the gym to dinner to a meeting to home to a few chores to bed, you allow no pause in the proceedings. If your mind starts to wander, you'll add some background distraction (music or TV). You're good at multi-tasking. Whatever the attack (type #1), you have no intention of slowing down to find out what it is.

8) <u>The</u> <u>Perfectionist</u>: You feel that if you don't meet a high standard, you are unacceptable (type #1). So you must be very skilled, very productive, very creative, very smart, very reasonable, very effective, very clever, very correct – or whatever hoop it is you must endlessly jump through to avoid the attack. But you can never win this game because, if you must perform to be acceptable, then you must not be acceptable to begin with.

9) <u>The</u> <u>Moral</u> <u>Perfectionist</u>: You must remain above the reproach of others (type #3). The slightest violation of your moral code could also bring on merciless guilt (type #1). For some, this pattern will include criticizing the "immoral" or "unethical" behavior of others (type #2). If your pattern is religious in nature, you might fear the judgment of God (type #3).

10) Very concerned with appearances: This is another form of perfectionism. Whatever you do must *look* good. Your house must be clean, your kids well mannered and well dressed, your marriage must look happy, you must appear to be successful and so on. And if you falter, others will think less of you (type #3). Some people specialize in just one area that must look good, while others have many.

11) Competitive: You feel high when you win because the attack (type #1 or #3) temporarily recedes. Without the attack, you would always feel like a winner.

12) Superior: You put yourself above others (type #2) to counter the hidden attack that puts you below them (type #1). This strategy does not eliminate the attack, just meaningful relationships.

13) Using a substance: You can use a substance to temporarily anesthetize discomfort caused by an attack. There are many possible substances such as alcohol, tobacco, caffeine, food, pain medication, illegal drugs, the computer, sugar, TV, spending, gambling, sexual experience, another person and chocolate. Since the anesthetic is temporary, the discomfort returns. So you must go back for more. This type of behavior can lead to a variety of unwanted consequences.

14) <u>Always</u> <u>right</u>: For some people, being right slows down the attack (type #1 or #3), but only for a while. So you must continue being right.

15) <u>Avoiding</u> <u>conflict</u>: Conflict (without an attack) is a common aspect of healthy relationships. To avoid it is to create distance. No matter, you will choose comfort first if conflict makes you feel unloved (type #3).

16) <u>Productive</u>: You must always be doing something you consider to be worthwhile. You feel that your value is measured by your actions. So if you were to waste time, your value would be diminished (type #1 or #3). You live with the pressure of having to continuously earn your worth.

17) <u>People-pleasing</u>: You make others feel good by smiling, being agreeable, supportive and helpful. Behind the scenes, you feel that if you are not pleasing, people won't like you (type #3).

five

DECEPTIONS

The "demon's" primary deception is that it hides below the surface and pretends that it does not exist. The second deception is that it focuses on something about you (your appearance, actions, income etc.) but actually attacks *who* you are. There are also some specific varieties of attack that can be deceptive and difficult to recognize. Here are a few examples.

1) The Double Whammy: Here, the "demon" will create some distress and then attack you for the distress it just created. "I was so nervous I couldn't even talk to her. What a loser I am." The "demon" caused you to be nervous (type #3) and then attacked you for it (type #1). "I'm so depressed I'm not worth anything to anyone." The "demon" created your depression (type #1) then attacked you for being depressed (type #1). "I feel guilty when I yell at my kids." The "demon" caused

you to yell at your kids (type #2) and then made you feel guilty (type #1).

2) The Self-Help Attack: "I'm such a loser for not working out regularly" (type #1). This is not the "demon" being motivational. It is simply using the situation as an excuse to attack. If anything, it demoralizes you and makes it less likely that you will start to work out regularly.

3) The Party Binge: Even though you are trying to diet, you eat a potato chip at the party because you are nervous (type #3). You then get attacked for the potato chip (type #1) which makes you feel bad, so you eat another. Which brings another attack, which makes you feel worse, so you eat a third, and so on. By the time the bowl is empty, you feel totally disgusting (type #1) and head for the brownies.

six

FEELINGS

In most cases, what alerts you to an attack is that something does not *feel* right. You might feel uneasy, nervous, down, irritated, embarrassed, upset, discouraged, defensive or guilty. At times, the feeling will not be clear enough to name. On the next page is a list of words that can help you identify such a feeling. As you read down the list, the words that catch your eye may name your current feelings. While these feelings could be entirely caused by the real world, it's also possible that they are a mixture of the real world *and* an attack.

So the feeling can be a starting point for finding the attack. Let's take "pressured" as an example. Bobby is driven to be the top sales person in his company. He would say, "I'm very motivated, that's just how

I am." But if we scratch the surface, Bobby feels *pressure* to outperform his coworkers. That pressure is discomfort. It comes from the attack that he really doesn't measure up (type #1). So Bobby must keep proving himself in order to neutralize the attack. The pressure actually feels normal to him, it's all he's ever known. Let's look at a few more examples.

<u>Hurt</u>: The real world component might be someone forgetting your birthday, which disappoints you. Then add the type #3 attack that the person doesn't care about you, and you now feel hurt.

<u>Abandoned</u>: Suppose you are renting a vacation house on the ocean with five friends, and when you return from walking on the beach, they have all gone off somewhere. Below the feeling of abandonment might be the type #1/#3 combo that you don't measure up to their standards.

<u>Unsupported</u>: Imagine telling your spouse about your boss being unfair, and your spouse siding with your boss. You could feel unsupported, but with an edge of resentment (type #2).

FEELING LIST

futile	rushed	pushed	frantic
mistreated	frustrated	tense	disgusted
lonely	sharp edged	embarrassed	overwrought
discouraged	powerless	unsettled	disgraced
degraded	used	squeezed	beaten
down	scattered	unsupported	neglected
jealous	vulnerable	inhibited	unimportant
blocked	foul	rejected	manipulated
pessimistic	dejected	exasperated	despondent
excluded	crushed	disappointed	defeated
lost	conspicuous	deserted	pushed
stretched	restless	muddled	passive
jumpy	intimidated	upset	offended
disheartened	cold	impatient	shy
disregarded	blamed	tired	hopeless
self-conscious	rattled	stuck	tentative
dismal	demoralized	abandoned	belittled
concerned	pressured	heavy	threatened
withdrawn	worried	burdened	suspicious
undesirable	overlooked	harassed	imposed upon
trapped	dominated	torn	put down
apathetic	overpowered	let down	hurt
reserved	disrespected	battered	aggravated
rigid	helpless	unwanted	nasty
cheated	betrayed	confused	apprehensive
gloomy	squashed	inadequate	raw
isolated	strained	wary	avoided
exposed	irritated	smothered	controlled
nervous	agitated	pressured	forlorn
wiped out	lethargic	abused	timid
melancholy	confined	slighted	empty
uneasy	exhausted	humiliated	ignored

When your system is under duress, the attacks can come more easily. The following are some examples of this phenomenon.

1) Stress: There are many causes of stress, such as pressure, demands, mistreatment, sensory overload and frustration. The pressure of rushing to be on time, for instance, revs up your body and makes it easier to overreact to anything that slows you down (type #2). The stress puts more wind in the "demon's" sails. Any form of stress will make it easier to react.

2) Stored anger: Anger stores up. You might carry anger dating back to childhood. Because stored anger is not visible, you would not know it existed if you did not intentionally seek it out. The internal pressure created by stored anger can make you more reactive,

so the attack (type #1 or #2) will be triggered more easily.

3) <u>Pain</u>: Pain can cause you to be more irritable (type #2).

4) <u>Tiredness</u>: Being tired can increase depression (type #1). It can also make you more irritable (type #2).

5) <u>Loss</u>: The "demon" can turn grieving (the natural response to loss) into depression (type #1). Grieving is the healing process, depression prevents it.

The stress response is a protective reflex that prepares your body for physical exertion (fight-or-flight). Imagine bees starting to swarm around your head. It's the stress response that gives you the instant energy to simultaneously flail your arms and run like hell. This same response can also be triggered chronically if you are under ongoing duress from financial pressure, continuous noise, a hostile work environment and so on. Your body simply idles too high. When this response is being triggered, if you do not work it off physically, you will accumulate stress.

In many cases, it is not the external event but your internal reaction to the event that triggers your stress response. For example, if your supervisor is talking to you disrespectfully, and your "demon" picks up on it, you might become fearful (type #3) or defensive (type #2). Both of these reactions (caused by the "demon") could trigger your stress response. If your "demon" were not activated, you might simply wonder what your supervisor's problem was. It would still be externally unpleasasnt, again like bad weather, but you would not take it personally and react internally.

Another example occurred just yesterday. I saw a client who came in because, a few days earlier, the build-up of job pressure finally left her sitting on the workroom floor crying with her heart racing. As we discussed the situation, she admitted to being a perfectionist. If she walked away from a job that was not done well, she would feel inadequate (type #1). So her supervisor was piling on work "that had to be done today," knowing that she would complete it. The real-world component was her supervisor piling on the work. But it was her "demon" that created the pressure to complete it. She knew she could not be disciplined for just doing a normal day's work. It was her "demon" that created most of her stress.

nine

PARENTS

Children normally inherit the "demon" from their parents. The culprit is often the type #2 attack. Here are several ways parents can unknowingly express this attack:

1) Tone of voice is the most common. If you tell your son for the third time to empty the dishwasher, and your voice has an edge to it, there will be a hit-word below the surface.

2) A second method of communicating the attack is through common expressions. Here are a few examples: "I am very disappointed in you." "Why can't you do anything right?" "Why can't you be more like your sister?" "What's wrong with you?"

3) A third variety involves having perfectionistic expectations. Whether your kids meet your expectations or not, they will grow up feeling that they are only good enough when they measure up to certain standards. This implies that they are never good enough just as they are.

4) The most harmful way to express the type #2 attack is through anger. I will elaborate on this in Part V.

You might look back at the list of ways parents can pass on the "demon" in the chapter "The Perils Of Childhood" (page 13).

ten

SELF-ESTEEM

High self-esteem is natural. It is inner attack that lowers it. When the attacks weaken, your self shines through your personality more brightly. You then automatically like and appreciate yourself more.

eleven

ILLUSION

If an attack is calling you "inadequate" from below the surface, you *feel* inadequate. Such an attack can continue your whole life, affecting your confidence, relationships, decisions and job opportunities. The attack has you under its spell. It has created the *illusion* that you are inadequate. If you could simply switch the attack off, you would blink, look around and wonder how you could have been away from yourself for so long. And you would feel elated.

To varying degrees, nearly all of us are living in a state of illusion.

twelve

CONSEQUENCES

The "demon" might actually create as much distress as the real world. It affects the personality of practically every person on the planet. It tampers with your moods, reactions, relationships, self-esteem, appreciation, comfort level...and so on.

Every aspect of your life can be influenced. Here is an example from a work situation. One of my clients came in complaining that, since she got a new supervisor six months ago, her life has steadily deteriorated. She said that he speaks to her disrespectfully, looks for reasons to discipline her, yells at her in front of other employees and treats her unfairly. He has written her up three times in the last four months, while in her previous 12 years with the company, she has never been written up and has gotten awards for being an excellent employee. Now she has started taking anti-depressant medication, feels nauseated going in to work, yells at her kids, and her relationship with her husband is strained. Her unhappiness has been created not only by the "demon" in her supervisor, but by her own "demon" as well.

Multiply this kind of pointless, needless suffering millions of times all over the world, and add in marital and family strife, domestic violence, divorce, childhood abuse, rape, teen suicide, depression, crime, terrorism, persecution – and so much more – and ultimately war. This is the magnitude of suffering created by the "demon".

thirteen

THE ATTACK IS PRESENT WHEN...

...you are in a bad mood
...you feel uncomfortable around others
...you doubt yourself
...you are inhibited, self-conscious or embarrassed
...you are down on yourself
...you are resentful
...you are defensive
...you are judgmental
...you are depressed
...you are irritated
...you are insecure, jealous or possessive
...you are prejudiced
...you have an attitude
...you are pessimistic
...you are shy or timid
...you misinterpret
...you take a joke seriously

...you are hard to please
...you worry about appearances
...you are controlling or demanding
...you deflect a compliment
...you need to win
...you crave attention
...you have to be right
...you are easily offended
...you need to be liked
...you require perfection
...you care (too much) what others think
...you need approval
...you overreact
...you lack confidence
...you are disrespectful or mean
...you need to be special
...you get angry
...you are in an argument

PART IV

STOPPING THE ATTACK

one

STOPPING THE TYPE #1 ATTACK

The "demon" is very good at what it does. It operates in your subconscious and knows the most effective way to attack you in every situation. The only thing in your favor is that the attack is always a lie. If you were to become aware of the language of the attack, you would know it's a lie.

Instinctively you know that *who* you are is not bad, defective or worthless. If I were to do a poor job in a counseling session, I might feel like a failure afterward. However, if I were to recognize that I am under attack, that I am being *called* a failure (as a person), I would know it's false. I can be a failure as a counselor, but not as a person. No one on the planet can be a failure as a person.

The problem is that while the attack is below the surface, you are unaware of it. You only notice how you *feel*. So the "demon" can get away with its lies undetected – and has been doing so your whole life.

The strategy for stopping the attack is very simple: recognize it.

The most common clue is some form of discomfort. This tells you that an attack *may* be present. I say "may" because the real world is also a source of discomfort. The question is whether your reaction is purely about the real world, or a combination of the real world and the attack. Frequently it will be a combination since the "demon" tries to use anything that occurs in the real world as an excuse to attack. With a little practice, you will be able to recognize what part of your reaction is about the real world (e.g. car trouble) and what part is caused by an attack (e.g "you're a loser for having such an old car").

Once you know that an attack is occuring, you can get it more conscious by finding the hit-word.

two

FINDING THE HIT WORD

Simply recognizing that the "demon" is after you will slow the attack down part way. Finding the hit-word will then slow it down the rest of the way. The more conscious you are of the attack, the more it slows down. What follows are a few methods for finding the hit-word.

Technique #1: Notice how you feel. If you feel like a *loser*, that's probably the hit-word. So say to yourself, "I feel like I am a _____" and see which hit-word fits.

Technique #2: The form of this method is, "_____ *therefore* _____," with the first blank being the excuse and the second blank being the hit-word. Examples: "She left me *therefore* I'm not worth loving." "I blew my presentation *therefore* I'm a loser." "My health is poor *therefore* I'm worthless." So when you are feeling down about something, apply this format and see which hit-word comes to mind.

Technique #3: Some people can access the hit-word directly by simply asking themselves what the "demon" is saying to them. Scanning the hit-word list can be helpful (page 31).

Technique #4: When you have some fear or doubt such as "They won't like me," there is usually an invisible second half of the statement that starts with *because*. Then comes the hit-word. The full statement might be, "They won't like me *because* I'm not good enough." Other examples: "I'll never be happy *because* I'm defective." "I can't do anything right *because* I'm incompetent." So whenever you notice yourself entertaining a doubt or fear such as the ones above, finish the statement with the most likely hit-word.

Once you know the hit-word, it may still take a while for the attack to lose momentum. You might temporarily find yourself *knowing* you are not a _____ but still continuing to *feel* that way. Stay focused and the attack will soon fade. You might slow the momentum more quickly by asking yourself, "Is it *true* that I am a _____?" This question will sharpen the focus of your mind.

three

STOPPING THE TYPE #2 ATTACK

When the Type #2 attack is firing, you will be able to feel a derogatory edge toward the other person. Sometimes it will be subtle. The more sensitive you are to how this edge feels, the easier it will be to catch the attack.

There are two varieties of this attack: reactive and ongoing.

Reactive: As the name implies, this variety of the attack involves reacting to something in the moment. A person makes a comment you don't like and you react critically. The best method I have found for unplugging this attack is to catch it when it is occurring, and simply think to yourself "stop" or "stop name-calling." Your brain is wired to react critically to a certain kind of stimulus. You are trying to re-wire your brain, to break the *habit*. You don't even need to know the hit-word. Some of you may not be able to break the habit completely, but will simply get better and better at catching the attack before it can develop. By saying "stop" or using some other signal (I just say "demon"), you can nip it in the bud.

Ongoing: This is a reactive attack that has become chronic. Someone criticizes you and for days you dwell on what the perfect comeback would have been. Or perhaps you are still resenting your neighbor for something he did six years ago. To break this type of attack, it is more helpful to find the hit-word you are directing at the other person, and then ask yourself if it is actually true. To find the hit-word, simply say to yourself, "He/she is such a _____" and plug in the first hit-word that comes to mind. Once you have done that, you are ready to tell yourself to stop. If the attack is a strong one, you may need to do this repeatedly for a while. Incidentally, I believe that the core of forgiveness is stopping an ongoing attack against the offender.

four

RECOGNIZING THE TYPE #2 ATTACK

Until you notice your type #2 attack, it will seem like the other person is the problem. The name-calling will seem like a factual description of the person. But once you catch the attack, you will realize that your reaction itself is causing most of your distress. Instead of simply seeing Rhonda as annoying, you recognize that your "demon" is using her behavior as an excuse to trigger your reaction of annoyance. Not liking her behavior is natural, but getting annoyed exaggerates your natural reaction.

One of my clients gave two examples from the previous week. In the first, she was at the library doing work in the reference room and a woman close to her was slurping on a sucker. The noise disturbed her to the extent that she got up and left the library. As we examined the situation, it was clear that the level of noise (decibels) was not stressful, so it must have been her interpretation of the noise that bothered her. It turned out to be the type #2 attack, that the woman was rude and uncouth. Another person might not have even noticed, thought it amusing or perhaps been mildly distracted. My client originally thought that it was a fact in the real world that the woman was uncouth. It was not until our session that she realized it was simply her judgment that upset her.

Her second example was also at the library. She was returning books that she knew were a day late, but she had never been charged a late fee for one day and assumed it was library policy. This time, she was charged a late fee of $1.10. This seemed unfair and when the librarian would not waive the fee, she got irritated, argued and eventually asked for the head librarian (who was not there at the time). By the end of this drama, both my client and the librarian were upset. Ironically, my client is a generous person who would gladly donate money to the library. Once again, she thought the problem was out there in the real world – the library was being inconsistent and unfair. In our session, she was able to recognize that the late fee made her feel accused of being negligent (type #3), and so she got defensive (type #2).

In order to stop this attack, you must first become aware of it. The feeling of being criticized can come in many forms. Look for feeling self-conscious, embarrassed, disliked, discounted or unwanted. Notice when you feel like you said the wrong thing and alienated the other person. Pay attention if someone tells you that you took what they said the wrong way, or that you are being too sensitive.

Once you suspect the attack, the next step is to find the hit-word. With this form of the attack, the way to become conscious of the hit-word is to ask yourself what the other person thinks of you (assume the worst). You could also use technique #2 from "Finding The Hit-Word." For example, "I'm laughing too loud *therefore* he must think I'm a jackass."

The third step is to remind yourself that it is your own attack that is causing your discomfort. Regardless of what the other person is thinking, it would not bother you if you had no attack of your own operating. You would not take it personally.

six

TIPS AND REMINDERS

The following are pointers that may help in your work to stop the attack.

1) Cultivate the concept that you are not alone. You have an enemy inside (the "demon") just waiting for an opportunity to attack. This will allow you to dispel the convincing illusion that you attack yourself. When you think, "I'm really down on myself today," shift to the perspective that you are *being* attacked. Once you do this, you are no longer simply caught in the quicksand of your feelings. Now that you have an enemy, you can muster yourself to oppose it.

2) Too many hit-words can cause you to lose focus. If several seem to apply in a situation, I would pick one and use it exclusively.

3) Do not bother trying to reason with the "demon" or to convince it that you are a good person. It doesn't care. Getting angry at it is equally futile. The "demon" is an *it* (not a *he* or *she*) and does not have feelings. It is not *part* of you, but simply a disorder. As such, it merely acts according to its nature, which is to attack. So there is nothing to be gained by interacting with it.

4) Know your profile. The better you know when and where you might be attacked, the easier it will be to recognize an attack as it occurs.

5) It will be useful to find little tricks to help yourself stay alert. You might post reminders at home, in the car and at work. Or perhaps keep a symbol of the "demon" on your desk. Carrying a notebook and writing the date and time whenever you notice an attack will also sharpen your awareness. Whatever works.

6) If you suspect that you are walking into a situation where an attack will be triggered, set your mind in advance to anticipate it. Then stay alert.

7) Another way to put your mind on alert is to say to yourself, "Don't let the 'demon' get hold of this." You can say this just prior to or in the midst of a situation.

There will always be adversity in the real world. The point is to not let an attack make matters worse.

8) The basic principle is: *when you recognize an attack, it slows down.*

9) It takes ongoing work to be able to recognize an attack when it occurs. How it *feels* can be a helpful signal. Each of the three types of attack will have a different feel to it. Sensitize yourself to each feeling so you will recognize it more easily.

10) To keep yourself focused on this work over an extended period of time, I suggest keeping a notebook. Every night before bed, take a few minutes to reflect and make notes about the day. Were there attacks? Did you catch them?

11) If someone is being blatantly disrespectful, the real world piece is that it will be externally unpleasant. By external, I mean that it is "out there" in the physical environment. It is unpleasant the way a foul smell would be unpleasant. If you have a reaction *internally* (e.g. you get upset), that is caused by your "demon". You are the emotional victim only of your "demon", not other people.

12) It is normal to occasionally not like what a person says or does. Allowing the type #2 attack to exaggerate your dislike simply increases your distress.

13) The type #2 and #3 attacks are the easiest to recognize. I therefore suggest working on them first. Any attack that you stop will slow the momentum of the "demon" in all areas.

14) If you don't recognize an attack for what it is, you will simply think it's factual.

15) The "demon" attacks your self. It is your natural enemy. It hypnotically weaves the illusion that there is something wrong with you. Your work is to dispel the illusion and live in the light of your own truth.

16) You either oppose the attack process…or you live it.

seven

THE TUNE-UP

Hit-words are not beliefs. You don't *believe* you are worthless. You just *feel* that way because, below the surface, you are being called worthless. It's a thought process, not a belief.

But occasionally I encounter a person who does consciously believe the attack and will say something like, "Yes, I really am worthless." If this is you, the strategy is to clarify your language in order to dispel the confusion. I call this clarification a tune-up.

<u>Step</u> <u>one</u>: Let's suppose that you believe you are a failure. List all of your reasons for that belief.

<u>Step</u> <u>two</u>: How do the above reasons justify your being a failure? We can grant that all of your reasons are true, and that indeed you might be a failure

socially, or in your profession, or as a parent, spouse, friend or breadwinner. But that is not what the attack is saying. It is saying that, because you are a failure in some *aspects* of your life, you are therefore a failure as a *person*. That statement is never true.

You cannot be defective at your very core. The "demon's" deception is to use something about you as an excuse to attack you *yourself*. Anything *about* you can be flawed, but not *who* you are. However, if you still solidly believe that who you are is a failure, you might go back to the chapter titled "Your Self" (page 23). Perhaps you have a different belief about the nature of the self.

eight

STRATEGY OUTLINE

TYPE #1 ATTACK
1. Recognize that an attack is occurring
    a. your clue will be a negative feeling or reaction
    b. remember that it will relate to some real-world situation
2. Find the hit-word
    a. use one of the techniques if the hit-word is not apparent
    b. remember that the attack is a lie
3. The attack should now begin to diminish

TYPE #2 ATTACK
1. Recognize that an attack is occurring
    a. your clue will be that derogatory edge you feel toward the other person
    b. remember that you will feel justified

2. Regarding the reactive version:
   a. tell yourself to stop name-calling
   b. be firm with yourself
   c. remember that you have decided to eliminate *all* type #2 attacks
3. Regarding the ongoing version:
   a. find the hit-word
   b. tell yourself to stop name-calling
   c. be firm with yourself
4. Remember that you are stopping the type #2 attack for your *own* sake

TYPE # 3 ATTACK
1. Recognize that an attack is occurring
   a. your clue will be feeling uneasy (embarrassed, self-conscious, offended, unwanted etc.)
   b. remind yourself that the criticism is coming from your own "demon"
   c. even if the other person *is* being critical, your uneasiness can only be caused by the attack of your own "demon"
2. Find the hit-word
   a. ask yourself what the worst thing is the other person could be thinking of you
   b. remind yourself again that it is your "demon" calling you this
   c. ask yourself if it is actually true
3. The attack should now begin to fade

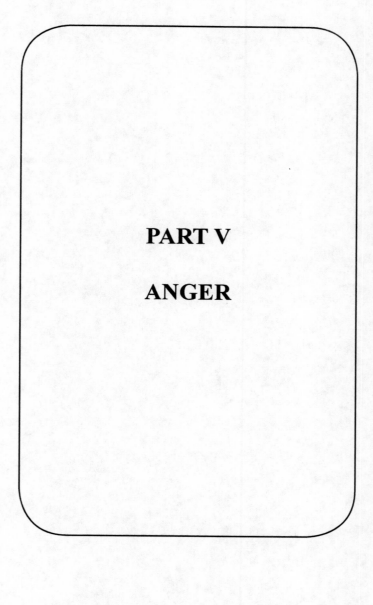

PART V

ANGER

one

THE ANATOMY OF ANGER

Anger is an alloy composed of four elements.

1) *The first element is the feeling of dislike.* What triggers your anger reaction is something you don't like. It might be something a person says or does. Your dislike, itself, is normal for you and not a problem. It can range from mild to very passionate and intense.

2) *The second element is criticism.* Anger, at its core, is name-calling, which is the type #2 attack (or #1 for anger against yourself). The attack itself intensifies into anger. It is the attack that gives anger a nasty edge. The actual language is usually hidden below the surface unless the name-calling becomes verbal. If you want to find the hidden language, simply say to yourself, "He/she is a real _____" and

then fill in the blank. The name-calling should come right up.

3) *The third element is aggression.* This is the primitive aggressive response present in many animals. When two dogs are fighting, they may look angry but it is only simple aggression. Anger requires name-calling and animals are too civilized for that. An animal can become aggressive when threatened, defending its territory, protecting its young or fighting for dominance. For humans, we would add anger to the list.

4) *The fourth element is adrenaline.* The physical counterpart of aggression is the fight-or-flight response. It is your body's primitive protective reaction when confronted with an external threat. Your body pumps up on adrenaline as it prepares for physical exertion (to fight or run). If you are on the sidewalk and a car hits a puddle in front of you, it is the fight-or-flight response that gives you the instant energy to jump out of the way. It is the same response that would fire if you were a letter carrier and a dog broke its chain and charged at you. When you are angry, fight-or-flight puts you into battle mode physically, which in turn puts you into battle mode mentally. You are then in no mood to resolve anything, you just want to win.

two

ANGER IS ALWAYS TOXIC

Since name-calling is toxic, and the core of anger is name-calling, anger is therefore toxic. Just as our goal is to eliminate criticism 100%, so our goal must be to eliminate anger 100%. This means that whenever there is a potential trigger (something you don't like), your intention would always be to not react with anger. You may never achieve 100%, but with that as your goal, it will be reasonable to bring your anger down 80%.

I realize that this is a challenge to the common belief that anger is simply a normal emotion that must be handled appropriately. "Appropriate" usually means to be moderate and not abusive. But name-calling is always abusive, so how can anger ever be appropriate? This discussion continues in the Appendix.

three

ANGER EXAGGERATES YOUR DISLIKE

When something you don't like triggers an anger reaction, your initial dislike gets exaggerated. So you
have amplified your original, normal reaction. You
have overreacted.

Further, when you dislike something, it will usually
affect your mood. The more you dislike it, the more
your mood is affected. So as anger escalates your
dislike, your mood gets progressively worse.

four

UP THE LINE

The chart on the next page gives a visual representation of the anger reaction.

STEP ONE: Something happens that you don't like. Not liking it is normal for you and not a problem.

STEP TWO: Your dislike turns critical (you get an edge). This is the type #2 attack. Two things happen at this stage: 1) Your dislike increases (becomes exaggerated) and 2) your mood gets worse.

STEP THREE: You escalate into irritation (mild anger). Four things happen at this stage: 1) Your dislike further exaggerates, 2) your mood gets even worse, 3) your adrenaline pumps your body into a mild fight-or-flight response and 4) you start to become aggressive.

STEP FOUR: You escalate into stronger anger. At this point your dislike exaggerates even more, your mood continues to degenerate, fight-or-flight grows stronger and you become more aggressive.

All of this can happen in a few seconds.

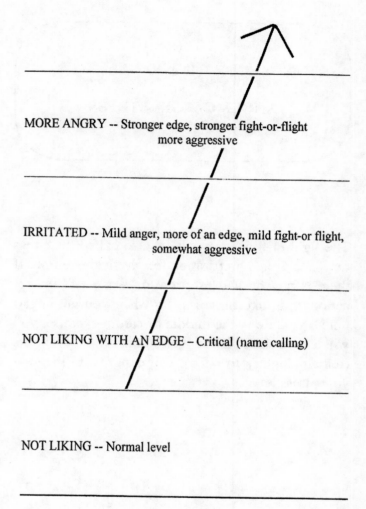

MORE ANGRY -- Stronger edge, stronger fight-or-flight
more aggressive

IRRITATED -- Mild anger, more of an edge, mild fight-or flight,
somewhat aggressive

NOT LIKING WITH AN EDGE – Critical (name calling)

NOT LIKING -- Normal level

As you go up the line, your dislike continues to exaggerate, your mood gets progressively worse, and you become increasingly more aggressive.

five

ANGER CAUSES STRESS

The fight-or-flight response is also called the stress response. It is a preparation for physical exertion. If there is no physical exertion to "work off" the reaction, you take in stress. So when you get angry, unless you are in the middle of cardio exercise, you will take in stress. If you then simmer for a few hours (remain slightly irritated), you continue to increase your stress level.

six

ANGER HAS A TARGET

You are always angry *at* someone or something. It is specific. It could be an inanimate object. The door sticks so you get mad and kick it. When you think you are angry at a "situation", the anger may resolve down to a specific person. You can be angry at something more abstract like an organization, but again, that may resolve down to a few people within the organization.

People occasionally tell me about a feeling they call "moral outrage" which might, for example, be about famine in some part of the world. If there is no name-calling imbedded in this feeling, then that is not what I am addressing in this book and not what I am referring to by the word "anger".

seven

SO YOU NEED ANGER TO...

Many people believe their anger is helpful in various ways. Here are some examples.

A. "It motivates me." Anger puts you in a worse mood and can make you impulsive and reckless. The real issue is why you are procrastinating in the first place. Are you depressed, overwhelmed, afraid, conflicted, worn out, lacking confidence? There are ways to get yourself moving that are healthier than the anger-adrenaline rush.

B. "If I don't release the anger, I will be pent up inside." If you don't get triggered in the first place, there will be no anger to release. However, when anger from the past has stored up inside, there are ways to release it privately. See the section on Anger Release in the Appendix.

C. "I need anger to get my point across," or "to get him to listen," or "to get her attention," or "to let him know that this is important," or "to let her know how strongly I feel." You may have trained the other person to ignore you until you are angry. It will be necessary to talk to the other person about listening to you without your having to resort to anger. This is an important issue but anger is not the solution. If the other person is your partner, you may need to address this in joint counseling.

D. "I need anger to let my kids know I mean business." Again, you may have taught your kids that they do not have to listen until you are angry. And your anger is name-calling which lowers their self-esteem and damages your relationship. So I suggest having a talk with them and explaining that you are trying to avoid anger, but that you still mean business. Then, if necessary, use consequences instead of anger to get their attention. If you stay in neutral when delivering the consequences, it will not lower their self-esteem. You might, in a calm voice, say "Kids, I have asked you three times now to clean up your room. If it is not done in 15 minutes, there will be no TV for two days. It's your choice."

eight

BUT IT'S JUST WHO I AM

No it isn't. No one is born short-tempered. You become that way. And so you have the option to change if you so choose.

nine

I AM JUST EXPRESSING HOW I FEEL

No, you are not. You are being verbally abusive. Anger is not a feeling, it is a reaction composed of the four elements listed in section one. The feeling in anger is dislike, which can be expressed without anger. It is an important part of your work to be able to distinguish between anger and dislike.

ten

USING ANGER

You can use anger to bully, intimidate, get compliance, control, repel or get revenge. But it is simply not worth it. You are poisoning your own mind, being verbally abusive, inviting repercussions and affecting your mood.

eleven

COSTS

Short term costs can be a bad mood, an argument, hurt feelings, violence, getting arrested or ruining a good time. Long term costs could be job problems, relationship damage, lost friendships, lowering the self-esteem of your children, depression or stress related issues (heart, immune system, TMJ, high blood pressure, asthma, colitis, fatigue etc.).

What's more, the costs come with no benefits. You get nothing of value from your anger.

twelve

SEPARATING DISLIKE FROM ANGER

The goal is to stay with disliking something rather than getting triggered up the line into criticism or anger. If you don't get triggered, your natural response will be to consider what you want to do about whatever it is. Some people are so accustomed to being triggered into an exaggeration of their dislike that they are not very familiar with simple dislike. It will be very useful to become familiar with the feeling. Perhaps you could first notice how it feels to have an edge in your voice or thoughts. Then, when you don't like something, pay attention to whether or not the edge is present. Remember, you can dislike something very intensely without being triggered.

thirteen

STOPPING ANGER

To stop an anger reaction means to not get triggered *internally*. To get angry on the inside and suppress it is of limited value. You will just store it up. The goal is to not get triggered at any level.

1. Alertness
There are no clever techniques for this. Anger is a habit. You are hard-wired to react just the way you do. Your reactions are fairly predictable. In order to weaken the habit, you must consistently interrupt the pattern. That means to be alert and catch yourself. You must be able to get in quickly and tell yourself to "Stop" or "Don't go there" or whatever phrase works for you. I suggest using the exact same words every time so that your maneuver to block the reaction, itself, gets wired in.

2. Quickness

You may only have five or ten seconds to block your reaction before you no longer want to stop. As the habit weakens, it will become easier to catch yourself. However, this is life-long work. Once you ride the momentum down, you will always need to maintain some level of alertness.

3. Go for 100%

Since anger is always toxic, the goal is to eliminate it 100%. That means your intent in all situations would be to not react with anger. You don't ever want to justify an anger reaction (e.g."Who wouldn't get angry at that?"). Anger usually feels justified. That's not the point. The point is that it is not in your best interest to go there. When you go for 100%, it will be reasonable to hit 80%, which is a significant reduction. But you will only hit 80% when you are actually trying for 100%.

4. More alertness

Alertness is the key to catching yourself. You are being alert for something to happen that you don't like. That's when you get in quickly and say whatever you have chosen as a block. If you miss the trigger and realize that you are angry, your only recourse may be to exit the situation. Regardless of the circumstance, staying there when you are angry will not be in your best interest.

5. Stay with dislike

The goal of your work is to stick with your natural reaction, which is to dislike whatever it is. Anger will only compound the problem. For example, if you are driving and someone cuts you off, you may not like it. But it's already done. If you get triggered, all that will do is make you dislike it even more, which will put you into a worse mood. So now, you have two problems: being cut off and being angry. By sticking with your original dislike, you are simply cutting your losses.

6. Motivation

To do this work successfully, your motivation needs to be around an eight or better (on a scale of 1-10). You can do this. I tell my classes that if I could give each of you a shock-collar that would fire when you got angry, your problem would be solved. All the shock-collar would do is increase your motivation to be alert.

fourteen

STRONG CLEAN LANGUAGE

Some people worry that without anger they will not be able to express themselves strongly. We will discuss strong expression in this section, but even so, you still may need to renegotiate what strong expression looks like with those you know. If you are being disregarded, you may need to address that concern as such. Anger is not an acceptable solution to the problem.

There are various ways to express yourself strongly. Your voice can be firm, emphatic, passionate or even loud. What is crucial is that your voice does not have a derogatory edge.

Without an attack, you can use strong language such as the following. "I detest what you did!" Or "I hate that you...." Or "I will not tolerate that!" Or "That is completely unacceptable!" Or "I can't stand the way you...." Again, monitor your voice tone. Strong expression can open the door to an attack. You may have to work at this for a while.

Another approach might be to say, "I need you to let me know that you understand how strongly I feel about this." Or "I don't think you get how strongly I feel about this." Or "What will it take for you to understand how strongly I feel about this?" As previously mentioned, when all else fails, you may need to address the issue of being disregarded in couples counseling.

PART VI

COUPLES WHO ARGUE

one

THE ARGUMENT

It is normal for couples to disagree, to have misunderstandings, or for one person to do or say something the other does not like. It's normal to want the other person to make changes. Since you are different people, there will always be disagreements and issues to resolve. Your work is to do it respectfully. Once you degenerate into an argument, your chances of resolving anything start to slip away.

The primary characteristics of an argument are a critical tone of voice and often anger. When you shift from a discussion into an argument, you become polarized and are no longer partners trying to resolve an issue. You are opponents, each merely trying to win. What you were disagreeing about becomes secondary and the battle itself takes center stage. Both of you are on the attack. If only one of you is on the attack, it is not an argument but simply verbal abuse.

During an argument, all three types of attack are usually operating. The type #2 and #3 attacks are the most obvious: you might feel attacked (type #3) and attack back (type #2). The type #1 attack is less noticeable. Partner's attack could make you feel bad about yourself but you don't recognize it because you are busy attacking back.

two

THE DESTRUCTIVE NATURE
OF AN ARGUMENT

It has been my experience in working with couples for many years that arguing, itself, is often the primary problem in a relationship. Many couples are unable to resolve even minor differences because they can't disagree without arguing.

There is no purpose to an argument, no point, no value. It is 100% destructive. You are simply calling each other names, either through your tone of voice or at the verbal level. The core of a good relationship is that positive energy you have with each other. How much arguing can your relationship endure before that energy begins to dissipate?

A relationship should be the center of your life, a source of happiness. Arguing takes you in the opposite direction. It can erode the intimate connection that is the primary source of your happiness.

three

ESCALATION

When you are already triggered and then get attacked, it throws fuel on the fire and you become triggered even more. The more you are triggered, the more aggressively you attack back. As your adrenaline level continues to pump up, your momentum to attack continues to increase. This is what happens to both of you as you are swept up into the escalation of your argument.

four

SIMMERING

Arguments don't generally end well. If you find yourself simmering after an argument, there is an ongoing type #2 attack that keeps you slightly irritated and ready to flare up again at the slightest provocation. While the goal is to avoid arguments in the first place, if you find yourself simmering, try to talk yourself down: "Stop name-calling, you are just hurting yourself," or "Don't let the 'demon' keep you in a bad mood." If that does not work, try exercise or distracting yourself in some way. There is also a breathing technique that may be helpful: breathe in through your nose and blow the air out slowly through your mouth as if you were blowing out a candle. As a last resort, try taking a cold shower (no, really).

fiive

YOUR INDIVIDUAL WORK
TO AVOID AGUMENTS

Once you intellectually understand how destructive agruments are, you will be more motivated to stop them. Your individual work is to prevent yourself from getting triggered. There are two types of potential triggers.

THE FIRST is for your partner to do or say something you don't like. Be alert! Alertness is 80% of your work. Remember the example of wearing a shock collar. All that does is make you alert. Once you catch a potential trigger, you must then step in quickly to block the criticism or anger reaction. "Stop, don't react," or "Stop, don't go there," or "Stop, back up and observe." This first response will buy you a few seconds to re-group. Find the most effective phrase to use to block your reaction. Then, as previously mentioned, use the exact same words each time. You eventually want that phrase to pop up automatically when there is a trigger.

Then, if you express your dislike to your partner, pay close attention to your tone of voice. You may also check inside to be sure your thoughts don't have an edge. You are both working to be free to express dislike or disagreement to one another without the fear of it triggering an argument.

Even when you are alone, your goal is still to avoid being triggered. Suppose you come home and your partner is out, but has done something you don't like. Immediately pay attention to your stream of thoughts – look for an edge. It is important to stay with disliking what your partner has done without exaggerating your dislike.

THE SECOND type of trigger is when your partner is speaking to you with a nasty tone of voice. Again, alertness is essential so you can recognize that he or she is triggered. Once you recognize your partner's attack, back up into observation mode. When you are observing how your partner is acting, you will be less inclined to take it personally and be able to see the attack for what it is. You will then be in a position to signal your partner (see next section).

six

YOUR JOINT WORK TO
AVOID ARGUMENTS

Your goal is to stay on the same side, to not attack each other. So you each must work to catch your own as well as your partner's triggers. Couples have an advantage over single people in that there are two of you paying attention. If one of you starts to get triggered, there are two of you to catch it. It can be easier to notice a tone of voice in your partner than in yourself.

When you notice that your partner has gotten triggered, you job is to signal your partner in a manner that won't throw fuel on the fire. I suggest the joint project of coaching each other as to how you each would like to be signaled.

THE FIRST TYPE OF SIGNAL is given when you notice that your partner has a critical tone of voice.

Be alert for this so you don't get triggered yourself and fire back. Then signal your partner in the manner he or she has requested. It could be "Do you notice an edge in your voice?" or "Do you feel triggered?" or "Did I just say something that triggered you?" It is imperative that the one who is signaled stop when the agreed upon signal is given and take a few seconds to check inside and then report back. "Yeah, sorry" or "No, I don't think so." If your partner says "no" you must simply trust and accept it.

When your partner signals you, try to step back and notice your tone of voice. Then pay attention to your body-reaction. Even if you are just in critical mode and not yet angry, it can still be a very physical experience. By focusing on yourself, the experience of being triggered becomes the object of your attention, rather than your partner. This can help you come down from your reaction.

THE SECOND TYPE OF SIGNAL is used when you notice that one of you is angry, or when the two of you are in a full blown argument. You call a time-out. I suggest using the time-out hand signal and saying, "Let's take a time-out and come back to this in 30 minutes." You must both solidly agree to comply with a time-out call without question. The 30 minutes allows your adrenaline to settle back down. During the 30 minutes, it is best to go into different rooms. Do not dwell on the argument during the time-out or you will keep simmering. Get on the computer, wash dishes, exercise – do something to distract yourself.

Some people will need more than 30 minutes to settle down. If you come back and start to heat up again, you have no recourse but to take another time-out.

It may require discipline to comply with a time-out signal, especially if you feel that your partner is just trying to avoid the issue. But comply you must! During an argument, there can be the illusion that you will resolve it if you hang in there. But the truth is, the nature of an argument itself tends to prevent any type of resolution.

seven

WHEN THE SIGNAL DOES NOT WORK

If your partner does not respond well to your signal, you have to decide what option to choose.

A) If you, yourself, are triggered, I suggest excusing yourself and leaving the room. "I need to cool down, I'll be back in 30 minutes."

B) If your partner is triggered and you are not, you could still excuse yourself and leave the room. "I know you don't want to take a break here, but I really need to. I'll be back in 30 minutes."

C) If your partner is triggered and you are not, you could stay in the room and drop into listening mode (see section 13). In listening mode, you simply pay attention and acknowledge what he or she is saying without agreeing or disagreeing. Mentally, you are observing your partner's attack without taking it personally. As you remain in neutral without fighting back, he or she will tend to de-escalate.

D) Stay with the argument. This is the option I would discourage.

eight

WHOSE "DEMON" IS IT ANYWAY?

Is your partner attacking you (type #2) or are you just imagining it (type #3)? This question can come up regularly. It takes a joint effort to find the answer. If you signal your partner and he/she is unable to detect an attack, then you might suspect that it is your own type #3 attack.

If the type #3 attack gets you on a regular basis, then you have some important work ahead. This attack is not easy to recognize by yourself because your focus is on your partner seeming to criticize you. Does your partner frequently tell you that you have taken what he or she has said the wrong way? Your work is to consider this feedback and try to determine whether or not your own "demon" is distorting your perception.

The antidote for this attack is to keep signaling your partner and trust the response. Behind a frequent type #3 attack is usually a strong type #1 attack. Your deeper work is to ferret that one out into the open.

nine

RE-INJURING YOUR RELATIONSHIP

If you injure your knee, you must protect it so you don't continue to re-injure it. Rest and freedom from further trauma are required for healing. Calling each other names, whether verbally or by tone of voice, creates injury to your relationship. The relationship will not begin to heal until you stop re-injuring it, until you stop the name-calling.

In a calm state, you would not believe or intend the names you implicitly or explicitly call each other. But in the heat of an argument, you fire at will.

Once you stop the name-calling, positive communication will begin to occur spontaneously. It is innate for each of you to be reasonable, compassionate and respectful if you are not on the attack. And softer emotions might then begin to surface such as hurt, sadness or fear.

ten

OLD ISSUES

Some couples have long-standing unresolved issues that continue to trigger arguments. If there has been a betrayal, for example, the question is whether the relationship is still viable. Resentment will interfere with finding that out. Resentment is an ongoing attack that runs in the background continuously. It can affect all of your interactions. Regardless of how intensely you dislike what your partner did, your resentment (name-calling) exaggerates it even further. Find the hit-word and tell yourself to stop it. You may have to do this repeatedly for a while.

Once the resentment has been stopped and you have returned to your normal level of dislike (no matter how intense), the two of you can then try to discuss the issue without it becoming an argument. It may still require alertness and signaling. The healing of a betrayal can be a long repetitive process, and you may need the help of a counselor.

eleven

RESOLVING ISSUES

There are many genuine couple's issues. Arguing is not one of them. It is just an obstruction. On the next page is a list of some common issues. Add to the list all of the small daily misunderstandings and disagreements that come up. Resolving these is an ongoing process. You both have the intrinsic tendency to be reasonable, compassionate and cooperative. So over the years, you would tend to get better at resolving your differences if arguing were not blocking your progress. Be mindful that some issues cannot be resolved, you simply differ. Recognizing that, you then work on accommodating and adapting to one another. It is the work of two different people sharing their lives with each other.

SOME COUPLES ISSUES

Parenting

Communication, listening, understanding, responding

Emotional contact, intimacy, being emotionally available

Appreciation, giving, being supportive, compassion

Forgiveness, healing the past

Energizing, re-romanticizing

Family, in-laws, adult kids

Depression, anxiety, illness

Finances

Betrayal, truthfulness, accountability, trust

Alcohol, drugs, other addictions

Domestic violence

Jealousy

Cultural or religious differences

Drifting apart, leading separate lives

Equality, control, domination

Codependency, dependency

twelve

COMMUNICATION STYLE

I decided to add this section and the next to give you a few suggestions on tuning up the quality of your communication. This work will not be effective until you have a handle on preventing arguments.

Communication style entails coaching one another on how you would like to be spoken to. Is your partner too abrupt, vague, careful, repetitive, crude, evasive or compliant? Does he or she interrupt and talk over you, or simply hog the conversation? When you pause, does your partner step in and start talking? Or does your partner not talk enough? Working on these issues must be a joint project. If you find yourselves unable to make progress, you might want to enlist the help of a couples counselor.

To listen and genuinely try to take in what your partner has to say is a form of giving. It does not entail agreeing but simply trying to understand what
partner is expressing. When you drop into listening
mode, it could be for a few seconds, a few minutes
or possibly half an hour. Here are the basic steps for
listening.

STEP ONE: pay attention. You are giving your full
attention and avoiding distractions and interruptions.

STEP TWO: put yourself on the back burner. Your
sole focus is on what the other person is saying. That
means not giving your own opinion, or advice or a
solution. It also includes not defending yourself, disagreeing or criticizing.

STEP THREE: give feedback. Feedback is best given as a short statement rather than a question. There are several types of feedback.

A) Paraphrasing. You are simply restating what you think your partner is saying or meaning. You can begin responses with words like "So..." or "In other words..." or "It sounds like...." Here are a few examples. "So when I said I didn't want to go, you took it personally." "In other words, you don't think I really care about your opinion." "It sounds like this whole problem revolves around not knowing how your mother will react."

B) Making an observation. Here, you are commenting on how your partner seems to be feeling or acting. "You seem confused as to which way to go." "You look nervous."

C) Making requests. In this case, it is OK to ask a question but only to request more information. "Could you say more about that?"

The listening process is self-correcting. If your feedback is not entirely accurate, your partner will correct you. "I am not actually confused, I'm just afraid that either way I go, it will end up a mess." Staying in listening mode will help your partner to express what he or she has to say. And your partner will appreciate that you are paying attention and trying to understand.

Many years ago, I was at a swimming pool with a friend and his five year old son. It was time to leave and my friend said, "Come on Evan, we have to go now." But Evan kept standing under a tree looking down and did not come. I went over and said, "It's no fun when you have to stop playing and go home." Evan nodded a little and started to come along. That was 10 seconds of listening mode.

fourteen

SUMMARY

There are four steps to this work:

1) Understand the nature of criticism and anger.

2) Understand the nature of an argument and the pointlessness of arguing.

3) Work to not get triggered into cricism or anger by your partner no matter what.

4) Work to signal partner when you notice that there is criticism, anger or an argument.

People generally find that once they stop arguing, they automatically start talking to each other more. That begins the healing process. The door is then open to work on creating the kind of relationship you both want.

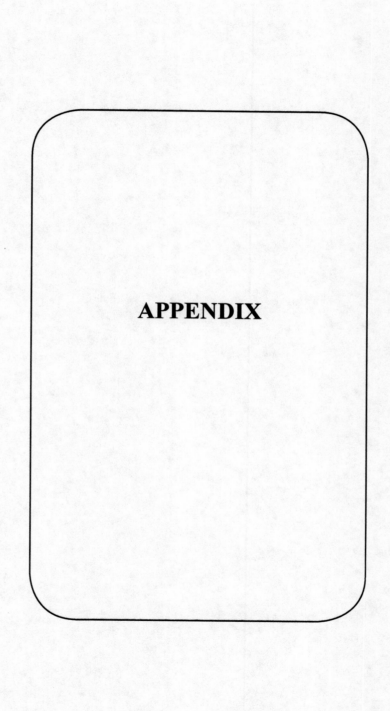

APPENDIX

appendix A

A NOTE TO THERAPISTS
REGARDING ANGER

Since the type #2 attack is toxic, it follows that anger carrying a type #2 attack at its core is also toxic.

This position will become clearer, and perhaps more reasonable, as I address objections that have been raised. But first, one clarification. When you are angry, your adrenaline is pumping. When you *say* "I'm very angry about that," but your body is calm, then you are not actually angry in that moment. You are either referring to anger that is stored up (but not activated) or you are simply saying that you do not like whatever it is. *Actual* anger is what I believe to be toxic. Stored anger is also problematic but needs to be addressed differently. See Appendix B for that discussion. Let's now look at a few objections to my position.

Objection #1: One therapist who works with trauma victims was rather vocal about my incompetence (type #2), assuming that I would tell such clients that they should not be angry. *Response*: When I am working with abuse/assault victims, I will help them to mobilize their anger regarding the perpetrator only for the purpose of helping them to *vent* that anger (initially in the session and later at home privately). This process is anger release and is done alone by choice, not reactively at another person. I do not view anger release as toxic (see Appendix B). Stored anger is part of the emotional damage from abuse. If a therapist supports the client's anger without helping him/her to release it, the client will probably end up with righteous anger that is chronic. This in turn can cause ongoing anger problems and depression.

Objection #2: Another therapist said that when working with a passive, dependent woman in an abusive relationship, she will try to mobilize the woman's anger so that the woman will have the motivation to take care of herself. The therapist gave this as an example of anger having positive value. *Response*: My focus would be on the woman's growth. To mobilize her anger without helping her to release it would not, in my opinion, further her growth. It might also trigger impulsive behavior rather than a thought out plan of action. And if she left him in anger, she might just go back when the anger subsided.

Objection #3: A third therapist said that he thinks anger is valuable as a signal that something is wrong. *Response*: I believe the genuine signal is *not liking* whatever you are angry about. This precedes the anger.

Objection #4: A friend of mine said that a person in her neighborhood was abusing his dog and the police would not take action. She said it was her anger that roused her enough to steal the dog and take it to someone who would properly care for it. This is the most common type of objection, someone thinking anger was helpful in a particular situation. *Response*: Anger can be toxic and still have secondary gains. The anger itself is still toxic. In the bigger picture, I don't think it serves you. There is a Samurai saying: "The angry man will defeat himself in battle as well as life." My friend went into battle angry and she was just lucky that her impulsive behavior did not backfire.

Objection #5: Occasionally, someone will say that it feels good to get overtly angry at the offender because it releases the pent up anger. *Response*: If you don't get angry in the first place, there is nothing to release.

appendix B

ANGER RELEASE

Anger that is not fully expressed stores up (from childhood on). Many people carry stored anger without knowing it. Once inside, it remains intact indefinitely, giving rise to a variety of symptoms. It can cause you to be quick-tempered, over-reactive or argumentative. It can contribute to stress, anxiety, post-traumatic stress, nightmares, high blood pressure and chronic depression.

The way to release anger is to *express* it. In my experience, a person cannot simply let go of it, or exercise it away, or work it through. However, expressing it to another person is toxic, ineffective and fraught with various forms of collateral damage.

So the best alternative is anger release – which is accessing and expressing the anger when alone. There are external and internal forms. External methods are outward and observable (e.g. Gestalt dialogue work, bat work, screaming). Internal release is not observable. From the outside you appear to be sitting quietly with eyes closed, but on the inside you are venting strong anger against the offender.

I started out using both forms of work, and then gradually began to favor internal release. For the past 15 years I have used internal release almost exclusively. I find it to be deeper and more exhaustive. I also find that it bypasses most resistance (inhibition caused by embarrassment) because a person can express strong anger with complete privacy.

Further, the anger expressed internally is just as real as the anger expressed externally. The benefits of the practice are typically global and observable. So while reactive anger has negative outcomes and is destructive, anger release has positive outcomes and is beneficial.

For more information, please see www.internal-anger-release.com.

About The Author

Allen Ross, LPCC, CEAP, has been in practice as a counselor for 34 years, and works primarily with anger-related issues. He has been teaching, training and presenting workshops in a variety of settings since 1966. Allen has conducted Anger Management classes at Riverside Hospital in Columbus, Ohio for the past nine years. He has also been a meditation teacher for 39 years.

Allen is currently in practice in Fairfield, Iowa and may be contacted at: angerwork@msn.com.

Ordering

This book may be ordered through most bookstores or at:

    www.amazon.com
    www.barnesandnoble.com

ISBN 978-057-808-4923

CPSIA information can be obtained at www.ICGtesting.com
Printed in the USA
LVOW05s0725250713

344360LV00001B/50/P